NATIONAL GEOGRAPHIC

T0308533

# Getting Home

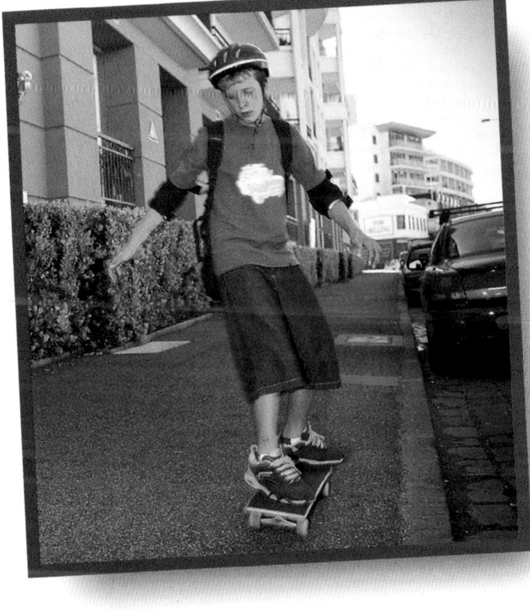

Leroy Taylor

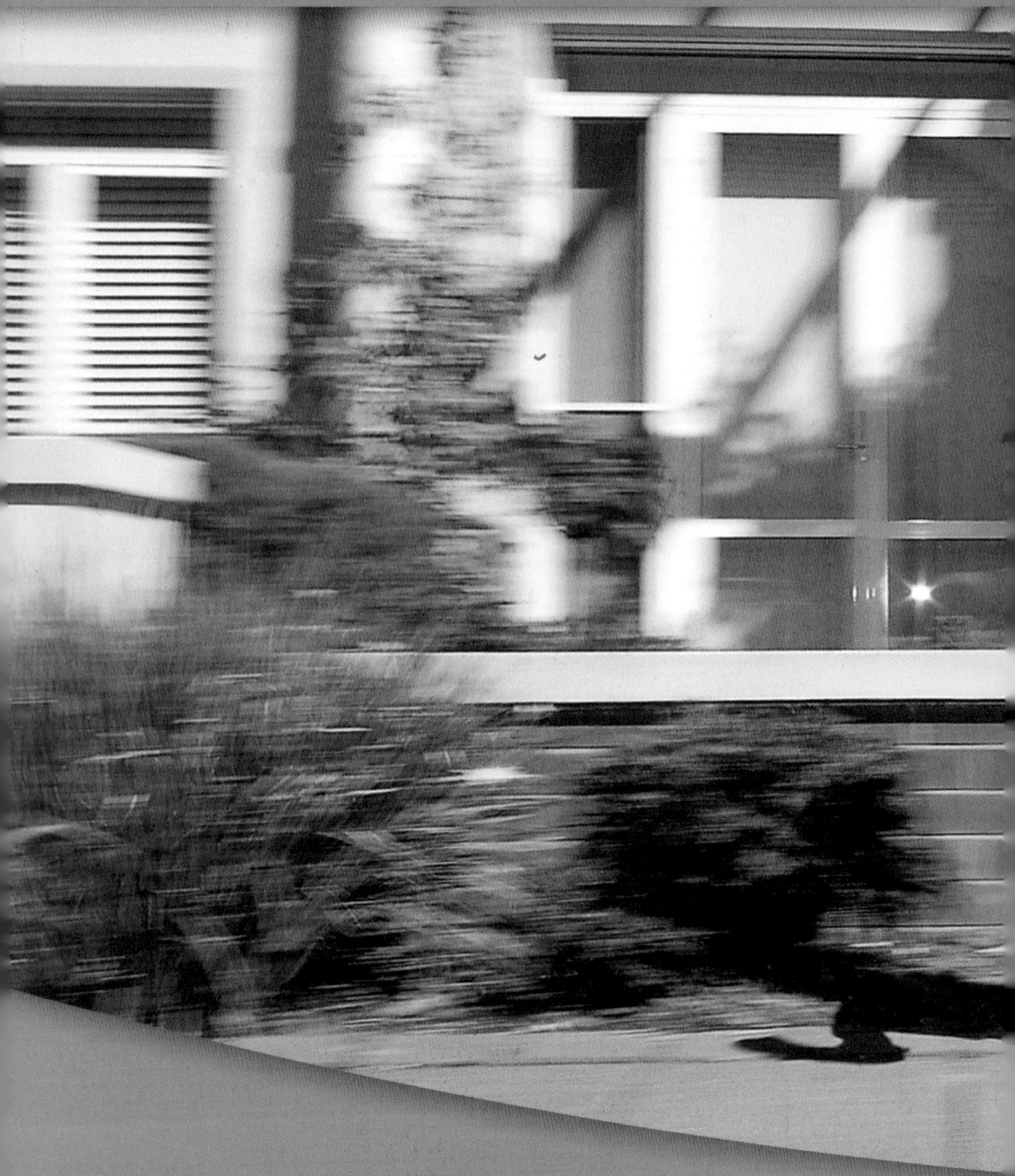

# 2 How do I get home?

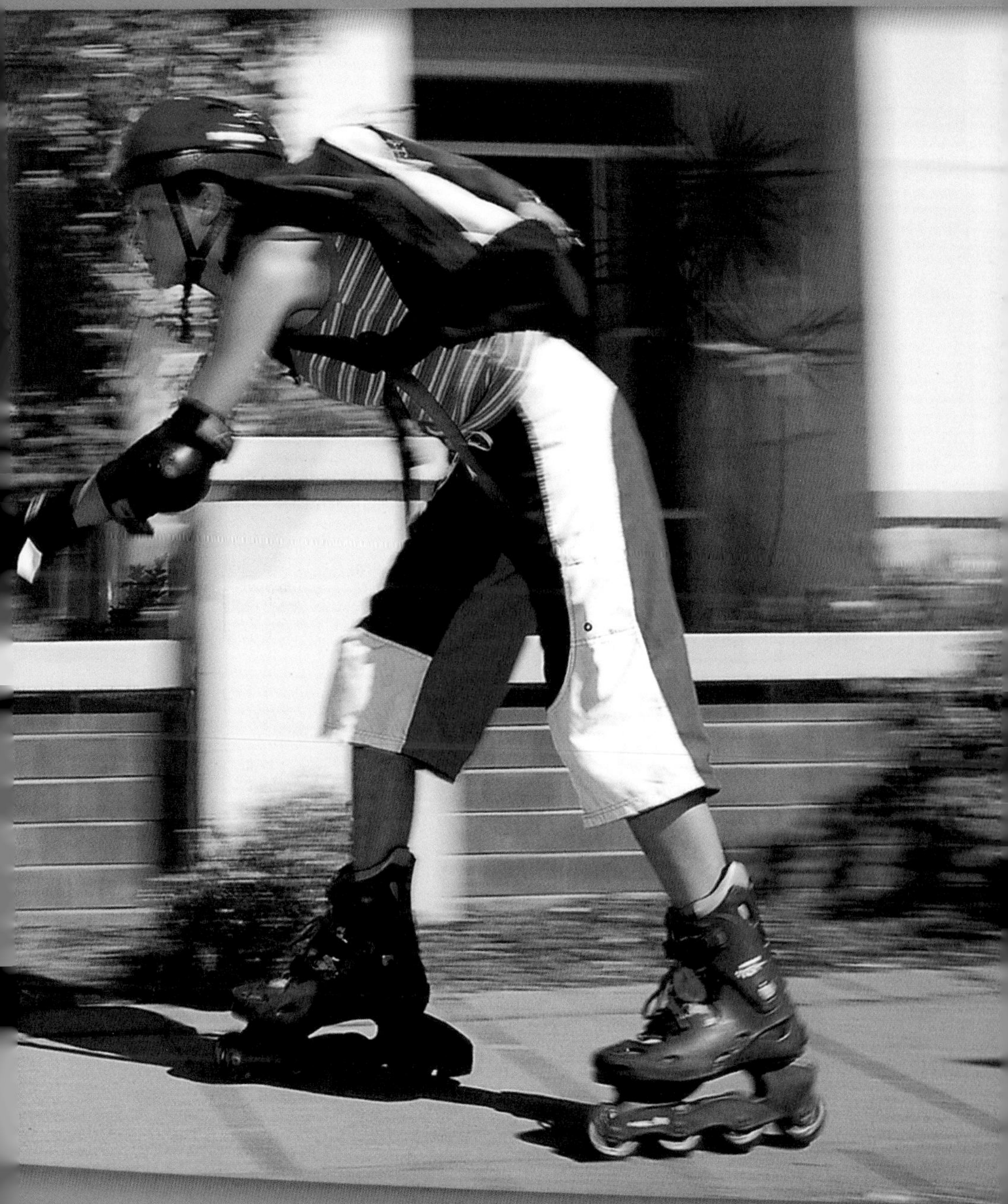

4

# How do I get home?

# 6 How do I get home?

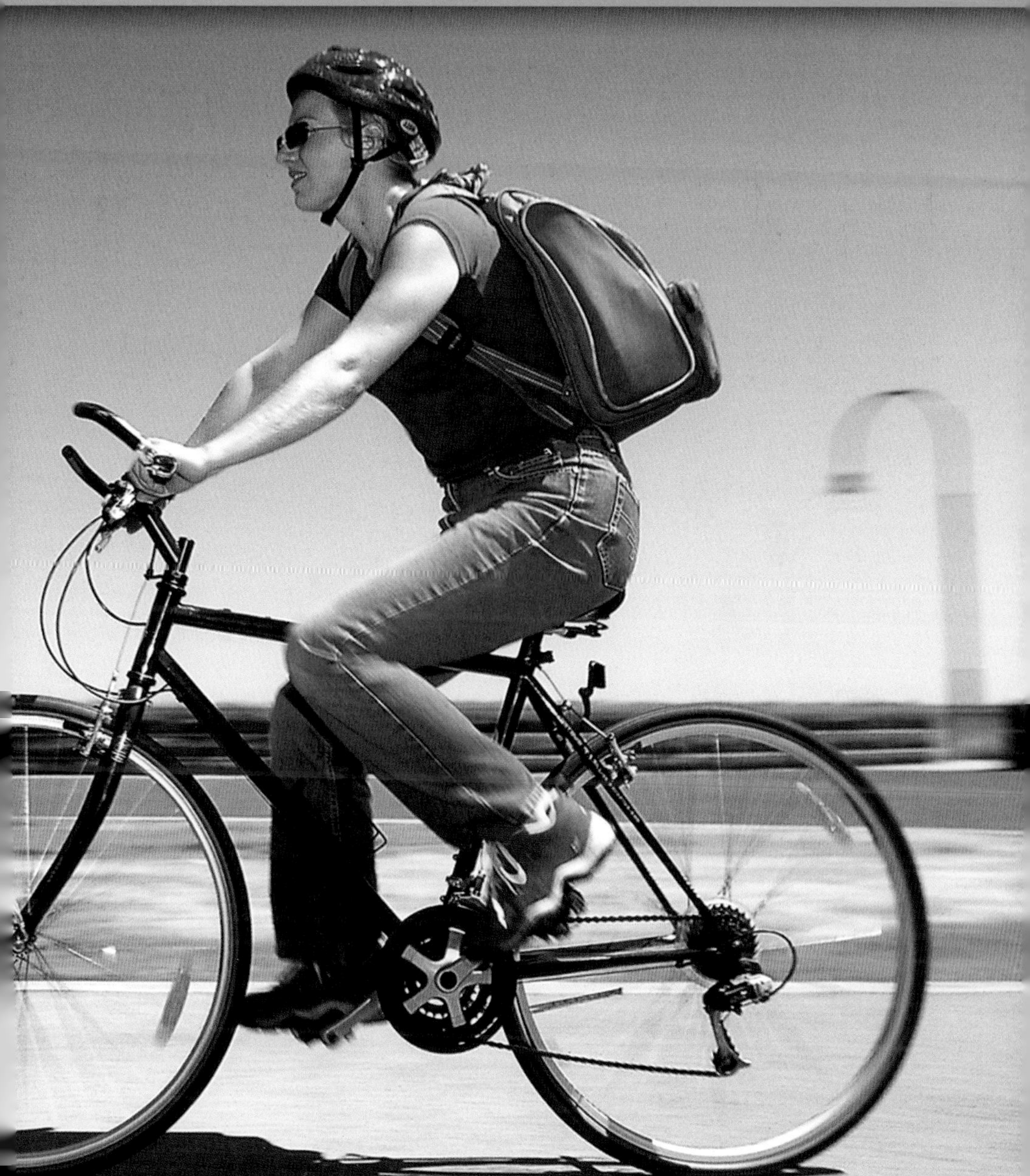

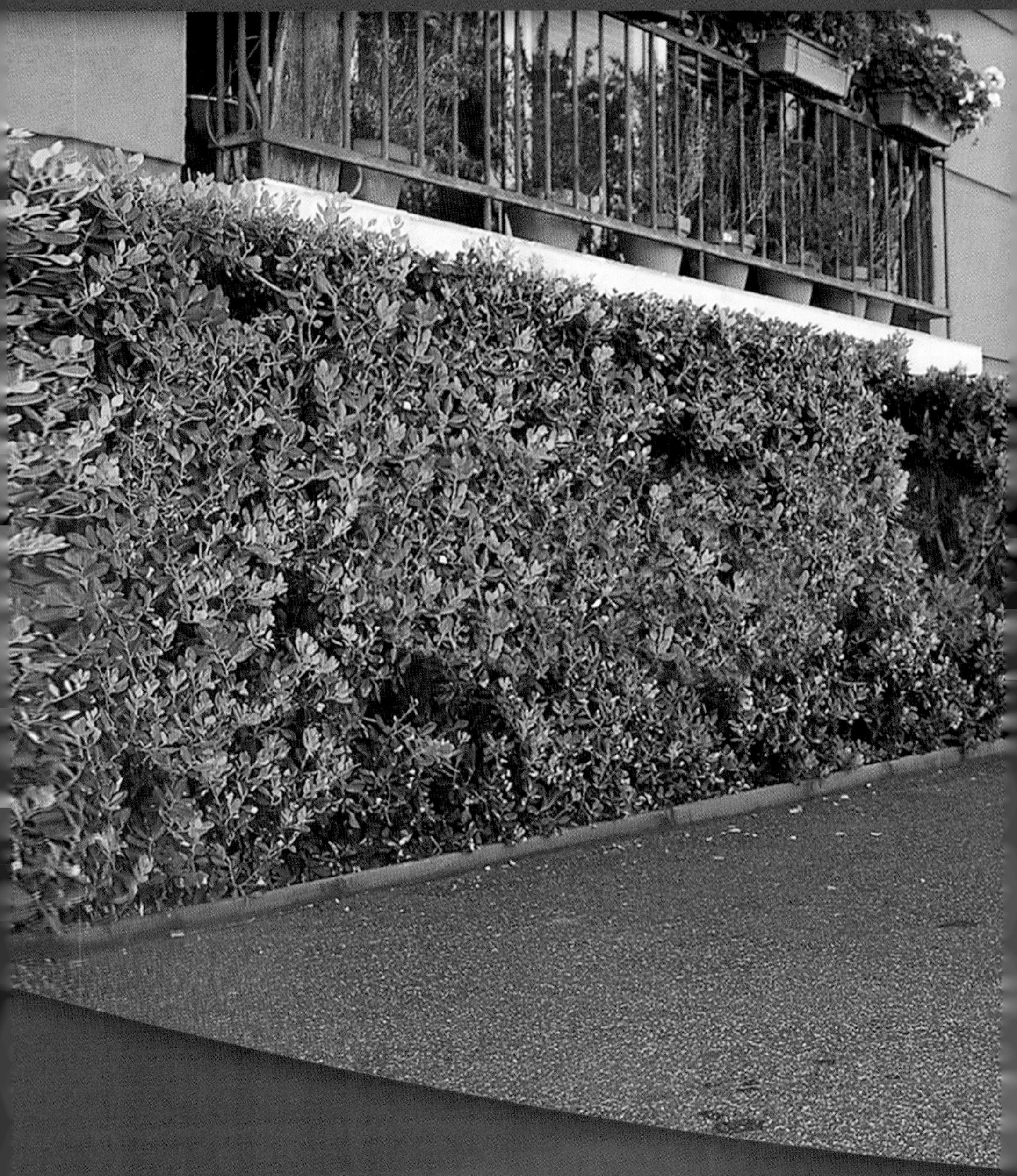



# How do I get home?

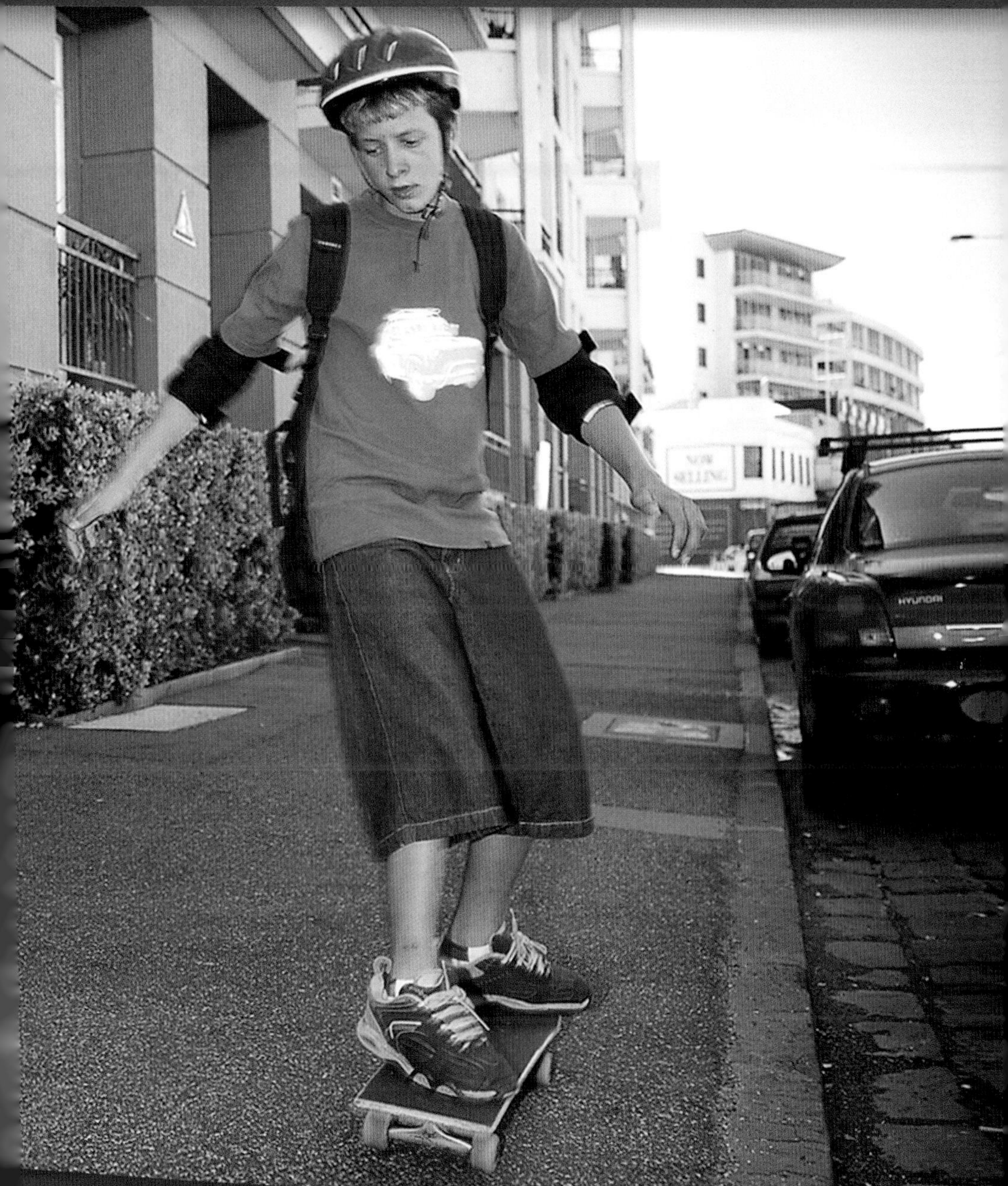
NOW
SELLING
HYUNDAI

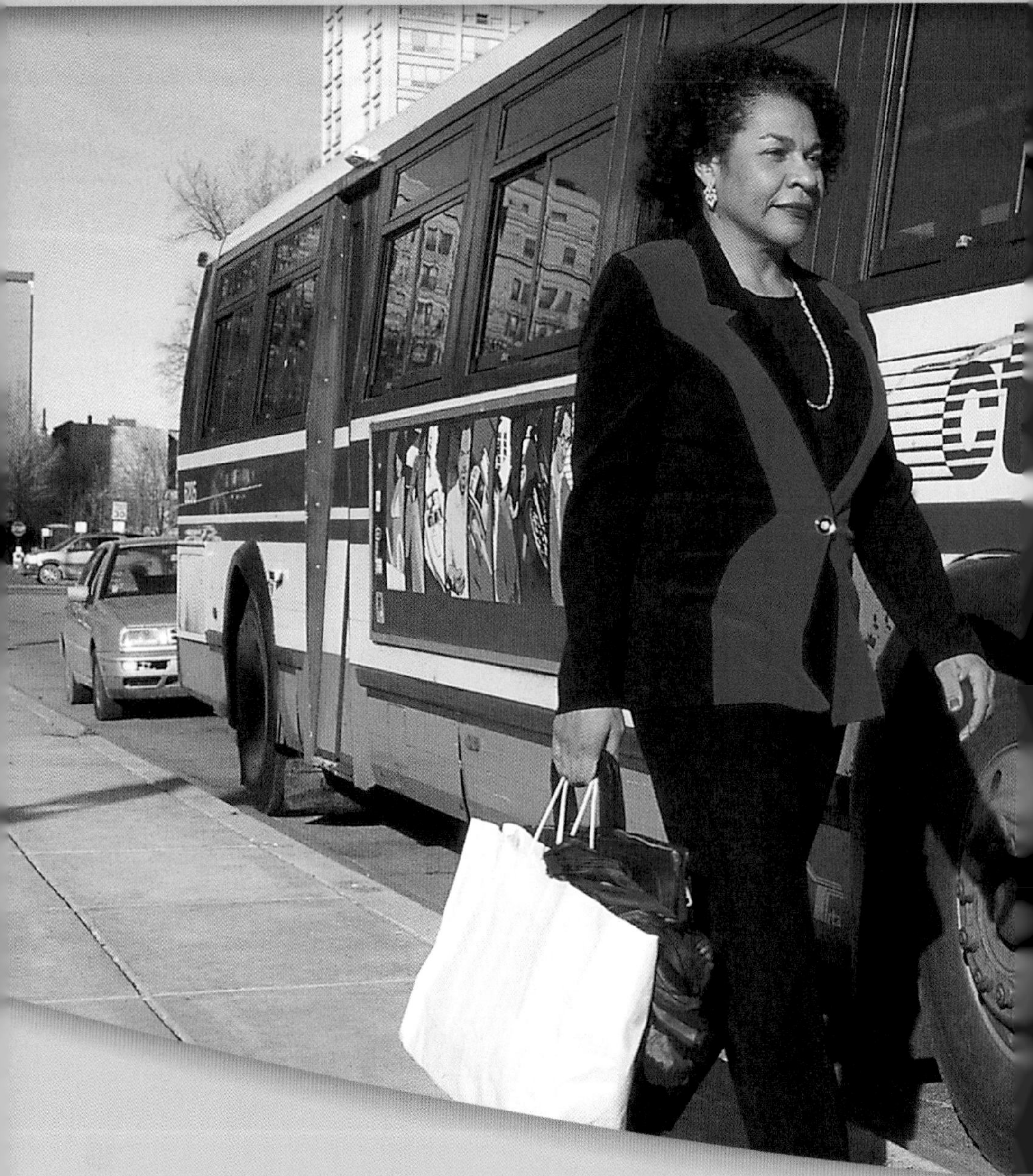

# How do I get home?

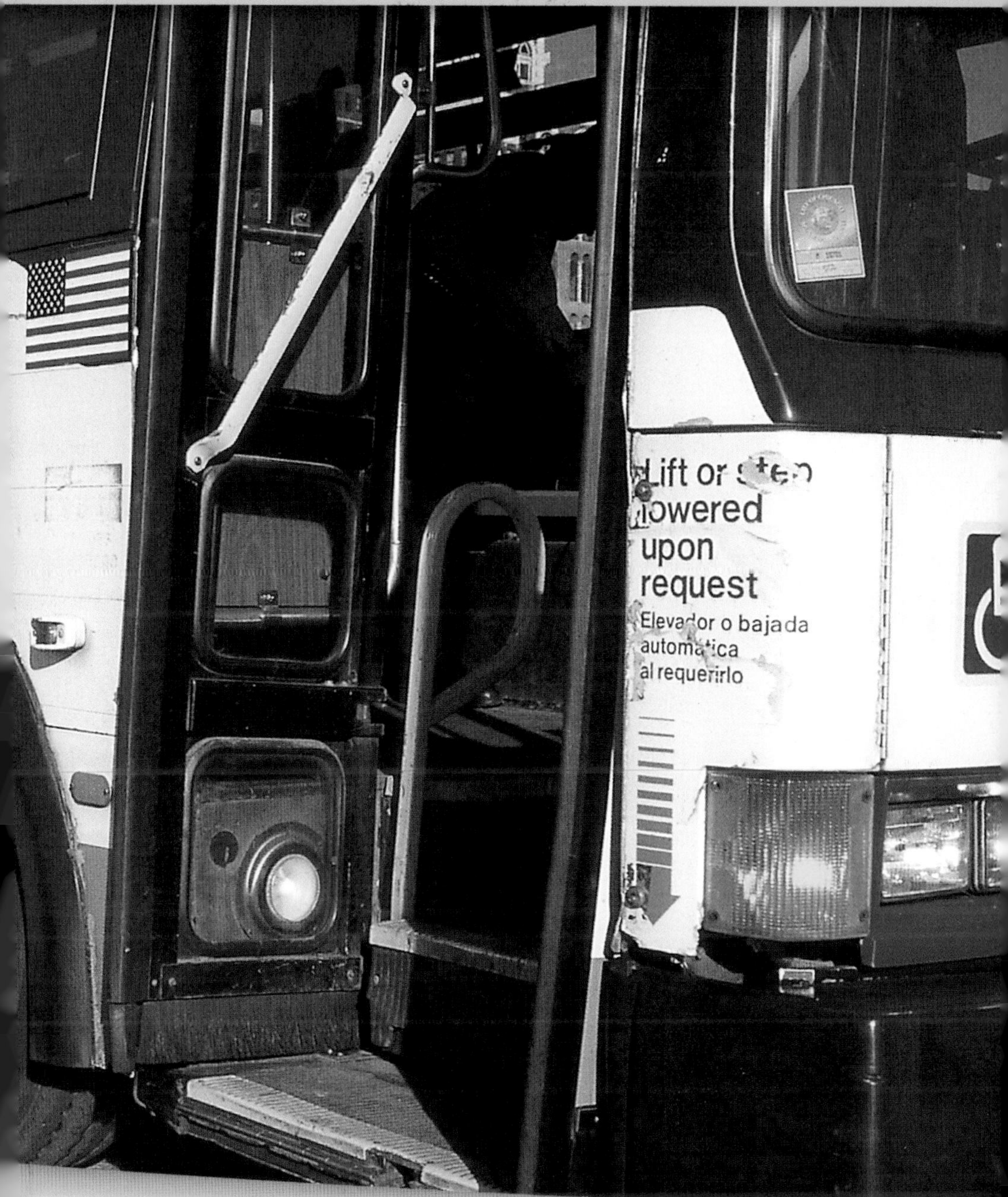
upon
request
Elevador o bajada
al requerirlo

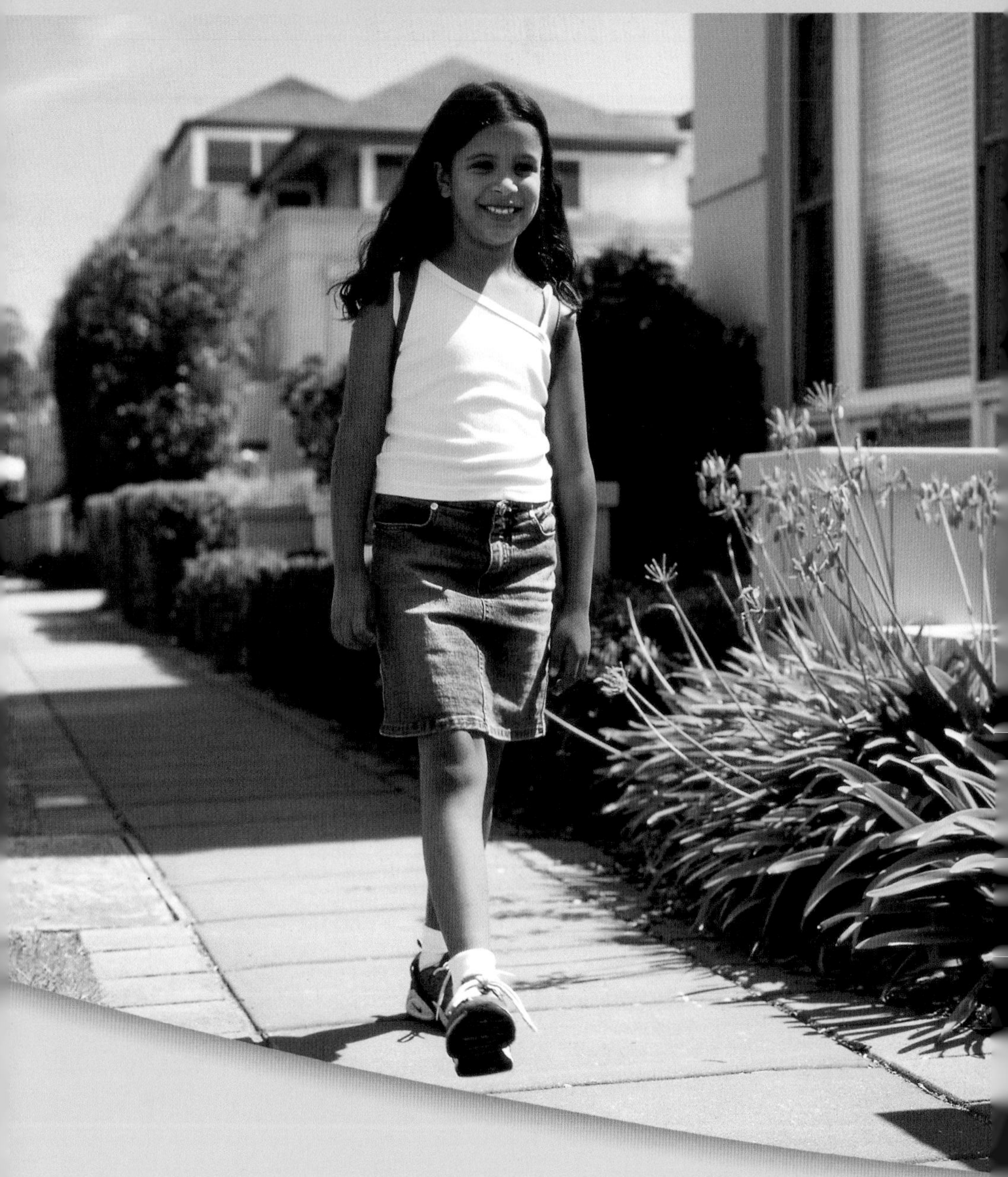



# How do I get home?